# Table of Contents

Introduction ........................................................................................................... 6

1. Bourbon Whiskey Cake for Damon ............................................................. 8

2. Blueberry Banana Pancake for Bonnie ...................................................... 11

3. Salted Potato Fry for Caroline .................................................................... 14

4. Bloody Mary for the Vampires ................................................................... 17

5. Jeremy Gilbert's Healthy Fruit Bowl .......................................................... 20

6. Cupcakes for Sweet Sheriff Liz .................................................................. 23

7. Roasted Eggplants for Elena ...................................................................... 26

8. English Breakfast for Klaus ....................................................................... 28

9. Bulgarian Cake for Katherine .................................................................... 31

10. Pizza for Elena's Sleepover ...................................................................... 33

11. Blueberry Omelet for Caroline's Pregnancy Cravings ............................. 37

12. Banana Cake for Sheila Bennett ............................................................... 39

13. The Vampires' Favourite Mimosas .......................................................... 42

14. Damon's New York Cheesecake .............................................................. 44

15. Thai Chip for Josette ................................................................................ 47

16. Double Cheese Burger For Humans by Damon.................................................. 50

17. Spiced Cupcakes for Stefan.................................................................................. 53

18. Chicken Salad Sandwiches for The Female Cast............................................... 56

19. Blueberry Slush for Bonnie .................................................................................. 58

20. Fish and Chips by Klaus ....................................................................................... 60

21. Sangria as Blood Substitute................................................................................. 63

22. Red Velvet Cupcake for The Vampires .............................................................. 65

23. Bread and Butter Pudding by Enzo .................................................................... 68

24. Brownies for A Vampire Get-together .............................................................. 71

25. Stuffed Bell Peppers for Elena's Slumber Party............................................... 73

26. Fake Blood Beetroot Puree.................................................................................. 76

27. Hot Steak Like Hot Stefan ................................................................................... 78

28. Curried Potatoes for Salvatore's Late Dinner................................................... 81

29. Bloody Wildcat Cooler Mocktail for Vampires................................................ 83

30. Bloody White Chocolate Bark ............................................................................ 85

31. Puff Pastry for Caroline and Stefan.................................................................... 87

32. Tasty Sandwich for Vampire Elena.................................................................... 89

33. Lime Curd for Lexi................................................................................................ 92

# Vampire Diaries Cookbook

Recipes to Turn into A Vampire

By: Lauren P.

Copyright © 2021 by Lauren P.

# License Notice

This work is protected by copyright law and is not to be copied in any form. Reproduction and distribution without the prior permission of the author are strictly prohibited. The contents of this book are deemed accurate after extensive research. However, the author will not be held liable for any damage resulting from the reader's interpretation of this book.

34. Skewered Chicken for Salvatore Brothers ......... 95

35. Bourbon Mocktail for Damon's Fans ......... 98

Conclusion ......... 100

Author's Afterthoughts ......... 101

About the Author ......... 102

# Introduction

The vampire diaries series was a treat to watch. The plot and the romance were perfect. They couldn't have picked a better cast for this show. People all around the world are fans of the show, this series birthed the desire in many people to turn into vampires. So, how about food inspired by this show? This cookbook is ideal for just that. Recipes inspired by scenes, characters, or the food present in the show itself, this cookbook has it all.

So, whenever you miss Vampires or any of the other characters, just turn to this cookbook. The recipes are so simple yet the dishes are extremely tasty. You could even cook some of these dishes as a snack to have while rewatching the show. You could get creative and adjust or experiment with a few of these recipes. Make any changes you like, as long as the dishes are to your liking.

# 1. Bourbon Whiskey Cake for Damon

Throughout the series, Damon has made it quite clear that he loves Bourbon. We could use this information and try and impress him. So, why not mix Bourbon Whisky in a cake? It is common to mix alcohol in cakes. It will taste amazing along with the chocolate, and the adults will surely love it. Just make sure you don't serve this cake to your children. This bourbon whisky cake surely will be your favorite.

**Ingredients:**

- 2 eggs
- 2 cups of sugar
- 1 tsp of salt
- 1 cup of sour cream
- 1/2 cup of vegetable oil
- 1 1/2 tsp of baking soda
- 2 tsp of vanilla
- 1 cup of cocoa powder
- 1/2 cup of brewed coffee (room temperature)
- 1/2 cup of bourbon
- 2 cups of all-purpose flour
- 1 tsp of baking powder
- 1/2 cup of semi-sweet chocolate chips
- Chocolate ganache to garnish (optional)

**Serving Size -** 8

**Cooking Time -** 1 hour

**Instructions:**

Preheat your oven to 350*F.

Grease a 19 by 13 baking dish. Keep it aside.

Bring out a large bowl and add the eggs, sour cream, vanilla, sugar, and vegetable oil. Mix the ingredients till they are well combined.

Gradually add the cocoa powder and pour in the whiskey and coffee.

Mix well and add the flour, baking soda, baking powder, and salt. Combine well to avoid lumps.

Add the chocolate chips and roughly stir them into the batter. Pour the cake batter into the baking pan or dish. Bake for about 35 to 40 minutes.

Once it is baked, allow it to cool. Remove the cake from the baking dish.

Pour the chocolate ganache over the cake and serve.

# 2. Blueberry Banana Pancake for Bonnie

Bonnie and Damon share a special bond through pancakes. And I can see why. They are quick and easy to make for a really tasty sweet treat. Pancakes are extremely tasty. They are so simple and leave room for experimenting with syrups and garnishes. Try making these yourself with basic kitchen ingredients. You can always add different sauces and topping to enhance the flavor of the pancake.

**Ingredients:**

- 1 cup of all-purpose flour
- 1 tbsp of baking powder
- ½ tsp of cinnamon powder
- ¼ tsp of salt
- ⅔ cup of milk
- ½ cup of banana, ripe and mashed
- 1 egg
- 2 tbsp of honey
- 2 tbsp of melted butter
- ½ tsp of vanilla extract
- A handful of blueberries (as per taste)

**Serving Size -** 6

**Cooking Time -** 20 minutes

**Instructions:**

Bring out a bowl and mix in flour, cinnamon, salt, and baking powder.

Take out another bowl and whisk mashed banana, honey, milk, vanilla, and butter. Now combine both the wet and dry ingredients. Whip it well.

Slice a few blueberries and add them to the batter. Keep a few aside to garnish.

Heat a pan over a medium-low flame. Once the surface is hot enough, grease it with butter or oil.

Scoop out the batter and pour it onto the pan. Let it spread by itself and cook for about two minutes. You should see bubbles forming on the surface.

Flip the batter and allow the other side to cook. Take it out once it is ready and grease the pan lightly again. Perform the same process for the rest of the batter.

Garnish with the remaining blueberries. Serve with maple syrup or whipped cream.

# 3. Salted Potato Fry for Caroline

Caroline loves Potato Fries or Chips. But why stop at that? There is so much more you can do with potatoes. This is an interesting recipe for frying thin round potato slices. They make great side dishes or snacks. This dish leaves a lot of room for experimenting with herbs and spices. Just follow the recipe, read the instructions and enjoy a delicious plate of potato fry.

**Ingredients:**

- 1 lb. of small potatoes
- 1 tbsp of vegetable oil
- 1 tbsp of olive oil
- 1 tbsp of rosemary, chopped
- 1 tsp of garlic powder
- 1/2 tsp of chili powder
- Salt to taste
- Black pepper to taste

**Serving Size -** 6

**Cooking Time -** 15 minutes

**Instructions:**

Scrub and wash off the first or mud from the potatoes.

Slice the potatoes about a quarter-inch thick. Bring out a bowl and put the slices of potatoes in it.

Season the potatoes with salt and pepper. Give it a good shake or stir in the bowl to mix well.

Heat both oil in a pan placed over a high flame. Add the potato slices and Sprinkle rosemary over them.

Let the potato slices cook for about five minutes, till they turn golden brown. Then flip the slices.

Cook for another five minutes. Season with chili powder garlic powder and stir. Serve hot.

# 4. Bloody Mary for the Vampires

Want to attract a vampire? But at the same time, you do want to use human blood? Try shaking a glass of bloody mary in front of them. Maybe you could get lucky and one of the less smart ones may fall for the trick. Jokes aside, Bloody Mary is a famous cocktail, which tastes splendid. Made from vegetables like cucumber and tomato, this cocktail may seem weird for some. But trying the drink is totally worth it. Go on and read the recipe.

**Ingredients:**

- 32 oz of tomato juice
- 8 oz of vodka
- 1 medium cucumber, peeled and seeded
- ⅓ cup of distilled vinegar
- 1 tsp of celery seed
- 1 tsp of Worcestershire sauce
- ½ tsp of hot sauce
- 1 tsp of black pepper powder
- 2 cloves of garlic, minced
- ¼ tsp of salt
- Lemon wedges
- Salt to rim the glasses
- Ice cubes to serve
- Olives to garnish

**Serving Size -** 4

**Cooking Time -** 10 minutes

**Instructions:**

Blend the tomato juice, cucumber, vinegar, vodka, and celery seeds in a blender.

Once smooth, add the Worcestershire sauce and hot sauce and blend at high speed.

Add the garlic, pepper, and salt and blend again to make sure all the ingredients are well combined.

Begin to rim your glasses with salt. Place the lemon wedges onto the edge of the glasses.

Fill the glasses with ice. Pour in the contents of the blender into the glasses.

Give the cocktail a good stir and garnish with olives to serve.

# 5. Jeremy Gilbert's Healthy Fruit Bowl

Going from a regular teen to a buff vampire hunter must mean a lot of exercises and healthy eating. Jeremy must have worked hard and tried to become fit. Is there any better way to get fit and healthy besides using fruits? It is tasty, naturally sweet, and leaves you feeling full. You can make it anytime for breakfast or an in-between snack.

**Ingredients:**

- 1 lb. of strawberries
- 1 lb. of fresh pineapple
- 12 oz of blueberries
- 12 oz of grapes
- 4 kiwis
- 3 oranges or mandarins
- 2 bananas
- 1/4 cup of honey
- 2 limes
- 1 1/2 tbsp of fresh lime juice

**Servings Size -** 10

**Cooking Time -** 25 minutes

**Instructions:**

Assemble all your fruits. Start by slicing the strawberries and grapes.

Chop the pineapple into bite-sized bits. Slice the bananas.

Peel the kiwi and chop them too. Add all these fruits into your fruit bowl.

Remove the zest of two limes and add it to a small bowl. Pour in the honey and lime juice, and mix well.

Drizzle the lime honey mix over the fruits and toss it.

Serve with cream or vanilla ice cream, if you like.

# 6. Cupcakes for Sweet Sheriff Liz

Sheriff Liz is one of the sweetest characters in the whole vampire diaries series. She was a recurring important side character. A character like this does deserve a sweet treat. Cupcakes are the easiest, sweetest fluffy dessert cakes to give anyone. They are easy to make and are everyone's favorite. The recipe below shows specifically how to make citrus and zesty cupcakes. Try making them once, you will love the cakes.

**Ingredients:**

- ½ cup yogurt
- 1 cup of all-purpose flour
- 1 lemon
- 1 orange
- 6 tbsp butter
- 2 tbsp of lemon juice
- 2 tbsp of orange juice
- 2 eggs
- ½ tsp baking soda
- Pinch of salt
- 7 tbsp sugar

**Serving Size -** 10

**Cooking Time -** 30 minutes

**Instructions:**

Melt the butter and keep it aside. Grate the zest of the lemon and orange.

Preheat your oven at 360*F.

In a small bowl, mix the yogurt, butter, eggs, lemon juice, and orange juice. Add the zest of the orange and lemon to it.

Sift the flour, salt, baking powder, and sugar in a large bowl and mix.

Add the wet ingredients into the large bowl and mix with a spatula or a hand mixer till it is well incorporated.

Fill the batter into your cupcake tray to more than half its level.

Bake the cupcakes for 20 minutes till the top of the cake is golden.

Let the cupcakes cool for a while and then serve with your favorite frosting.

# 7. Roasted Eggplants for Elena

In some parts of the series, it has been made clear that Elena enjoys eggplants. Even though Damon hates it. This all for a good eggplant recipe. Roasted eggplant has a good ring to it, doesn't it? You can have this dish as a meal by itself or a side dish to any meat meal. The recipe for this is quite simple and easy. The dish itself tastes so good; you have to give the recipe a shot.

**Ingredients:**

- 2 medium eggplants
- 3 tbsp of olive oil
- 1/2 tsp of salt
- 1/2 tsp of black pepper
- Garlic powder to taste (optional)
- Onion powder to taste (optional)

**Serving Size -** 4

**Cooking Time -** 35 minutes

**Instructions:**

Preheat the oven to 452*F. Line a baking tray with parchment or butter paper

Cut the eggplant into bite-sized cubes. It should be an inch and a half thick.

Place the cubes in a large bowl. Sprinkle salt and pepper over them.

Toss the cubes to spread the seasoning evenly. Season with garlic powder and onion powder if using.

Place the cubes on the tray, spreading them evenly. Set the oven on roast mode.

Let the eggplant cubes roast for 20 minutes. They should shrink and turn caramel brown by the time they are ready.

Take them out and let them cool for a while. Serve hot.

# 8. English Breakfast for Klaus

Klaus is partially English, from what we know. And although he does have tendencies to act like a tsundere, he probably does miss English food. So, what better than a classic English Breakfast? It is simple, healthy, and extremely delicious. You can easily enjoy a wonderful morning with this as your breakfast plate. Assemble all the ingredients, follow the recipe and enjoy a plate yourself.

**Ingredients:**

- 1 cup of baked beans
- 4 slices of bacon
- 4 pork sausages
- 6 oz of mushrooms
- 2 tomatoes, cut in half
- Salt to taste
- 2 slices of black pudding
- 2 slices of white bread
- 4 eggs
- oil to grease

**Serving Size -** 2

**Cooking Time -** 35 minutes

**Instructions:**

Preheat your oven to 200°F. Keep a large baking dish in the oven, allow it to become warm. This is to keep all the ingredients warm.

Add the beans into a saucepan and heat them over medium-low flame.

Place a pan on a medium flame. Fry the bacon and sausages. Once brown and crisp, take them out and set them aside.

Sauté the mushrooms in the melted bacon fat till they are light brown. Transfer into the oven baking dish.

Sprinkle salt over the tomatoes and add them skin side up into the same frypan.

Add the black pudding and let cook each for 2 each side. Once cooked, add them to the baking dish.

Toast the bread slices in the pan, till brown and crisp. If needed add some oil. Take out the slice and fry the eggs, sunny side up or however, you like.

Place all the ingredients on a plate, with the bread slices served at the side.

# 9. Bulgarian Cake for Katherine

Katherine is our Bulgarian Witch. Acknowledging her culture and cuisine, let's make a Bulgarian cake called Grash Cake. This cake is usually made without any flour. It is a bit tricky, but the taste is totally worth it. You will crave for more after just having one bite of this cake. Gather all your ingredients, follow the recipe and enjoy a delicious slice of this cake.

**Ingredients:**

- 9 eggs
- 3 cups of raw walnuts
- 2/3 cups of Brown Sugar
- 1/4 cup of shredded coconut for decorating
- chocolate ganache for decorative coating

**Serving Size -** 10

**Cooking Time -** 1 hour

**Instructions:**

Begin by separating the egg whites from egg yolks. Preheat your oven at 350*F. Lime an 8 inches baking pan with parchment paper.

In a blender or a processor, pulse the wall-nuts and brown sugar till they are fine and no longer coarse.

Whisk the egg white to form soft and firm peaks. Mix and fold in the walnut and sugar mixture into the white.

Make four portions of this batter. Bake each part of the batter for 15 minutes to form separate layers of the cake.

Place a layer of the cake and coat it with ganache. Place another layer and repeat the process of coating.

If you like, use a piping bag, and coat the chocolate ganache all over the outside of the cake. Finally, sprinkle grated coconut and serve.

# 10. Pizza for Elena's Sleepover

Elena has a few sleepover party scenes with just the girls. Ordering pizza and just chilling with you girls sounds fun, right? But now it is time to level up. How about making pizza with your friends? Sounds tough? Don't worry, it isn't, at least not with this recipe. Follow the instructions and enjoy a pan pizza. You can modify this recipe to make the pizza according to your liking.

**Ingredients:**

- 3 1/4 cups all-purpose flour
- 1/2 cup cornmeal
- 1 1/2 tsp salt
- 2 tsp honey
- 2 1/4 tsp instant yeast
- 1 1/4 cups of water
- 3 tbsp melted butter
- 3 tsp oil
- 4 tbsp softened butter
- 1/2 chopped onion
- 4 minced cloves of garlic
- 28 oz tomatoes (crushed)
- 1/2 tsp sugar
- 1 tsp oregano
- 1/4 tsp red chili flakes
- salt as per taste (for the sauce)
- pepper as per taste (for the sauce)
- 4 cups of mozzarella cheese shredded
- 1/4 cup of parmesan cheese grated

**Servings -** 12

**Cooking Time -** 1 hour 50 minutes

**Instructions:**

Combine the cornmeal, yeast, salt, flour, and honey in a bowl. Gradually add the water, and melted butter. Mix the ingredients well to form a dough for about 2 minutes.

Using a spatula or your hands, knead the dough till it has a smooth shiny surface and doesn't stick to the sides of the bowl.

Knead the dough into a ball and place it in a greased bowl. Cover with plastic wrap and set it aside to rise for an hour.

Preheat your oven at 420*F and grease 9 inches round pans.

Roll out the dough into a rectangle 15 inches long and 12 inches wide. Brush the softened butter over the rectangular dough.

Roll the dough to form a cylinder. Press the dough down to make an 18x4-inch rectangle and cut it in half.

Fold the dough into thirds and pinch the ends together to form a ball for each half rectangular dough. Cover and refrigerate them for 45 minutes.

For the tomato sauce, heat oil in a pan, over a medium-high flame. Sauté the onion and garlic for 5 minutes. Add oregano, pepper, salt, and chili flakes, and let the sauce simmer for 20 minutes.

Roll the dough out into a circular shape and place it into the baking pans. Let the sides of the dough have about an inch of height.

Pour 1 1/4 cup of sauce with 2 tablespoons parmesan and 2 cups of mozzarella cheese per pizza.

Bake for 30 minutes, and then allow the pizza to cool down before serving.

# 11. Blueberry Omelet for Caroline's Pregnancy Cravings

People tend to have the weirdest of cravings when they are pregnant. It is safe to assume that Caroline did so too. Here is a recipe for a very rare sweet and savory omelet. A lot of women crave it. The taste of this omelet, however, is not bad, whether you are pregnant or not. Make the dish and judge yourself. You may find yourself making this omelet often if you have a sweet tooth.

**Ingredients:**

- 2 tsp of vegetable oil
- 4 large eggs
- 1 tbsp of coconut aminos
- 1 tsp of cinnamon powder
- 1/4 tsp of black pepper
- 1/2 tsp of salt
- 1/2 cup of fresh blueberries

**Serving Size -** 1

**Cooking Time -** 15 minutes

**Instructions:**

Beat the egg in a bowl using a fork or a whisker. Add the cinnamon powder, pepper, coconut aminos, and salt.

Place a frying pan over a medium flame. Pour oil in it.

Add the whipped eggs and let them cook for 3 minutes.

Add the blueberries over the eggs, evenly distributing them. Reduce the heat and bring it to a low flame.

Cook the omelet for 6 minutes. Check to see if the egg sticks to the pan using a spatula. Flip to cook the other order side for some time.

Transfer the omelet to your serving plate and enjoy.

# 12. Banana Cake for Sheila Bennett

Sheila Bennett is one of the sweetest grandmas anyone could ask for. Bonnie is a very lucky girl to have her. I can bet that Sheila was one of those grandmothers who used to bake a fresh warm Banana Cake for young Bonnie. Who doesn't love a fresh warm banana cake? The recipe for making Banana cake is very easy and the ingredients are easily available. So, bring out all the ingredients, and start baking.

**Ingredients:**

- 2 1/2 cups of all-purpose flour
- 5-6 oz of buttermilk
- 7 tbsp of unsalted butter
- 2 eggs
- 1 pinch salt
- 4 bananas
- 3/4 cups of brown sugar
- 1 cup of sugar
- 1 tbsp of baking soda
- 1/2 cup of walnuts

**Serving Size -** 12

**Cooking Time -** 1 hour

**Instructions:**

Preheat your oven at 350*F. Line a bread or loaf baking pan with parchment paper.

Bring out a bowl and mix sifted all-purpose flour, baking soda, and salt.

In another bowl, whisk the butter with both brown and white sugar. Add the eggs one by one to the cream beaten butter.

Whisk to mix well and then add peeled bananas into the batter mix. Add the flour and buttermilk and mix again.

Mix till there are no lumps and the batter is smooth. Now, add the walnuts.

Pour into the loaf pan. Bake for 25 to 30 minutes. Allow it to cool before serving.

# 13. The Vampires' Favourite Mimosas

There are many scenes where vampires enjoy the occasional glass of mimosas. The drink seems to cheer and lighten their mood up, especially during a tough situation where drinking real hard alcohol would be considered careless. Besides, mimosas are refreshing to have, especially on a hot, sunny summer day. So, go ahead, make this delicious cocktail for a party or a get-together. You surely will love this drink.

**Ingredients:**

- 3 cups of orange juice, chilled
- 1 bottle of dry sparkling wine, chilled
- 1/2 cup of Grand Marnier

**Serving Size -** 8

**Cooking Time -** 5 minutes

**Instructions:**

Bring up your serving glasses. Clean and wash them.

Fill each glass with 1/3 cup of dry wine. Now, add and mix 1/3 cup of orange juice to it.

Add a tablespoon or two of Grand Marnier. Give the drink a good stir.

Add additional ice if needed and serve chilled.

# 14. Damon's New York Cheesecake

Damon visits New York a lot. It also happens to be the place where he turned into a vampire. That is enough of a reason for me to include a famous dish from New York. Everyone knows and loves this cheesecake. You cannot help but have a bite of it whenever you see the creamy, smooth, white cake.

**Ingredients:**

- 1 1/2 cups of graham crackers
- 2 tbsp sugar
- 1 1/2 tsp vanilla extract
- 4 1/2 tbsp melted unsalted butter
- 32 oz cream cheese
- 1 1/8 cups of sugar
- 2 tbsp cornstarch
- 4 eggs
- 1 egg yolk
- 1/2 cup of heavy cream
- 1 teaspoon lemon zest

**Servings -** 12

**Cooking Time -** 1 hour 50 minutes

**Instructions:**

Add the graham crackers to a food processor and pulse them finely.

Preheat your oven to 350*F. Cover a 9-inch baking pan with foil.

Bring out a bowl and mix the melted butter, 2 tbsp sugar, and cracker crumbs. Empty the contents into the baking pan and spread them evenly on the bottom surface.

Bake the crust for 10 minutes and let it cool. Readjust the temperature of the oven to 425*F.

Whip the cream cheese using a spatula or hand mixer till it is smooth. One by one add sugar and cornstarch. Beat the cream in between.

Now mix in the eggs and vanilla extract. Throw in the zest and beat till it is smooth and lump-free.

Pour the cream cheese mixture into the baking pan. Bake at 425*F for ten minutes. Bring down your temperature to 227*F and bake for an hour.

Let the cake cool in the oven for another hour and then refrigerate for 12 hours.

# 15. Thai Chip for Josette

Josette loves Thai food. It is her favorite cuisine and she always orders Thai. Now there are various meals and dishes of Thai food out there. But this dish is one of the simplest and very easy to make. Another bonus is that you can make it as a snack, or a whole meal. These chips usually go well as a side dish with a slightly bland and not overpowering main dish. Read the recipe very carefully, follow the instructions and enjoy a plate of this starter dish.

**Ingredients:**

- 3 to 4 large potatoes
- 1 tbsp of Thai red curry paste
- 1 tbsp of chili sauce
- Salt to taste
- 3 to 4 tbsp of Coconut milk
- 1 Lemon
- 3 tsp of honey
- Lemon juice to serve

**Serving Size -** 4

**Cooking Time -** 35 minutes

**Instructions:**

Wash and scrub your potatoes. You can either choose whether you want to work with the peels on or off.

Slice the potatoes into wedges to the thickness of your liking.

In a bowl, mix the Thai curry paste, chili sauce, coconut milk, and salt.

Throw in the potato wedges and mix the paste well over the potatoes. Use your hands if required.

Grate the zest of the lemon over the wedges and give it a mix.

Drizzle the honey evenly over them. Air fry the wedge at 400*F for about five minutes.

Bring the temperature down to 350*F and fry for another 5 minutes. Sprinkle some lime juice over the chips and serve.

# 16. Double Cheese Burger For Humans by Damon

Damon quite often mentions burgers and how humans love burgers. Well, don't we all? A burger is one of the tastiest fast foods that exist. As long as we don't live off of them, eating a burger now and then won't cause a dent in your health. And who says that burgers have to be from a fast-food joint? You can very well make a delicious burger at home. Follow the recipe instructions to make the perfect Double Cheeseburger.

**Ingredients:**

- 1 hamburger bun
- ⅓ lb. of ground beef
- 1 pinch salt
- 4 processed cheese single slices
- 1 tbsp of salad dressing
- 1 slice of tomato
- 1 leaf of lettuce
- 1 slice of onion

**Serving Size -** 1

**Cooking Time -** 10 minutes

**Instructions:**

Cut the bun in half and toast it over a medium flame on a pan.

Split the ground beef into two halves and mold out thin patties from the halves.

Season the patties with salt and fry them for two minutes on each side.

Place two slices of cheese on each patty and let it melt.

Once the patty is cooked, take the pan off the stove.

Now we begin assembling the burger. Place the base bun onto your serving plate. Then place the dressing, followed by the tomato and lettuce.

Place a beef patty and then the onion. Now place the other beef patty and finish it off with the bun.

# 17. Spiced Cupcakes for Stefan

If given a chance to talk about Stefan, any vampire diaries fan would probably write an essay or a book about him. And we all understand why. Stefan has a sweet side but can be very bold and protective when he needs or wants to. Not to mention how good he looks. His whole personality reminds me of Spiced Cupcakes. Just like him, they are sweet with a few spicy moments in between. The taste doesn't disappoint and making them is always worth it.

**Ingredients:**

- 1 ¼ cups of all-purpose flour
- ½ cup of brown sugar
- ½ cup of white sugar
- 3 cups of powdered sugar
- ½ cup of unsalted butter, room temperature
- ¾ cup of cold unsalted butter
- ½ tsp of baking powder
- ½ tsp of baking powder
- ½ tsp of cinnamon powder
- ½ tsp of nutmeg
- 2 eggs
- ½ cup of sour cream
- 3 tsp of vanilla essence
- 1 tbsp of heavy cream
- pinch of salt

**Servings Size -** 12

**Cooking time -** 35 minutes

**Instructions:**

Grease your cupcake tray and preheat the oven at 355*F

Combine the flour, salt, cinnamon, baking powder, baking soda, and nutmeg in a bowl.

In another bowl, mix brown sugar with ½ a cup of white sugar.

Heat ½ a cup of butter in a saucepan till it turns light brown. Make sure you keep stirring it to avoid burning the butter.

Add the butter into the sugar bowl and mix well.

Add the eggs into the bowl one at a time and whisk well. Then add 1 teaspoon of vanilla extract to it.

Now gradually and slowly add the dry ingredients part by part, and whisk. Throw in the sour cream and whip it all together into a smooth batter.

Fill the cupcake tray with the batter and bake for 18 minutes. At 350*F

Now for the frosting, whip the cold butter and two cups of sugar for 3 minutes.

Add 2 tsp of vanilla extract and whisk with high speed.

Add the rest of the sugar and beat it for 2 minutes.

Decrease the speed and add the heavy cream. Whisk till for another minute or two.

Fill the frosting in a piping bag and frost the cupcakes once they have cooled down.

# 18. Chicken Salad Sandwiches for The Female Cast

The whole cast of Vampire diaries looks stunning and fit. The female cast is no exception. In fact, they keep looking better as the season progresses. It must take real hard work and a healthy diet to look and be fit. A chicken salad sandwich sounds just right. The tasty chicken paired with all vegetables is the perfect way to stay healthy. Go on, gather all your vegetables and chicken, and start making this tasty Chicken Salad Sandwich recipe.

**Ingredients:**

- 1 1/2 cups of cooked chicken (shredded or chopped)
- 1/2 cup of stalk celery, (chopped)
- 1 small onion, finely chopped
- 1/2 cup of mayonnaise
- 1/4 tsp of salt
- 1/4 tsp of pepper
- 8 slices of bread

**Serving Size -** 4

**Cooking Time -** 15 minutes

**Instructions:**

Bring out a bowl and add mayonnaise to it.

Now add in the chopped celery and onions. Mix it well using a fork.

Throw in the shredded or chopped pieces of chicken. Using the fork, mix the pieces evenly.

Sprinkle the pepper and salt over the chicken salad and mix it again.

Spread the chicken salad over a salad and place another slice over it. Do the same for the rest of the slices.

# 19. Blueberry Slush for Bonnie

Here is a blueberry Slush for one of the important characters in Vampire Diaries. The recipe for making this thick drink is easy. In fact, it is so simple, you can make it anytime and as often as you want. The best part about this recipe is that it takes only two ingredients to make it. So, hurry up, gather the ingredients, read the instructions carefully, and follow the recipe to enjoy this tasty slush.

**Ingredients:**

- 2 cups of frozen blueberries
- 1 ½ cups of orange juice
- Extra blueberries to serve

**Serving Size -** 2

**Cooking Time -** 7 minutes

**Instructions:**

Add the frozen blueberries into a blender or mixer.

Blend once or twice. Gradually pour the orange juice into the blender.

Blend till it is smooth but still a bit icy.

Now add the slush into your glasses. Add more ice if you prefer it super chilled. Top it off with some fresh blueberries to serve.

# 20. Fish and Chips by Klaus

Given his origin, Klaus must know how to make Fish and Chips like how he knows the back of his hand. This dish is tasty, especially for seafood lovers. It serves as a very good starter in many by-the-beach restaurants or shacks. People around the world love the combination of fried fish with chips. The recipe for making it is quite easy as long as you follow the instructions properly.

**Ingredients:**

- 4 large potatoes
- 1 cup of all-purpose flour
- 1 tsp of baking powder
- 1 tsp of salt
- 1 tsp of black pepper powder
- 1 cup of milk
- 1 egg
- 1-quart vegetable oil to fry
- 1 ½ lb. of cod fillets

**Serving Size -** 4

**Cooking Time -** 40 minutes

**Instructions:**

Peel and cut the potatoes into strips. Place them in a bowl filled with cold water.

In another bowl, mix the flour, salt, pepper, and baking powder.

Pour in the egg and milk and begin whisking. The batter should turn smooth and set it aside for 20 minutes.

Heat the oil in a large pot to 350*F. Deep fry the potatoes till they are crisp on the outside but soft on the inside. Place them on kitchen towels.

Dip and coat the fillets in the batter. Deep fry them one by one until it is golden brown. Take them out and place them on kitchen towels.

Place the potato chips and the fish on your serving plate and serve immediately.

# 21. Sangria as Blood Substitute

Want to be a cool vampire just like the ones in vampire diaries? However, you don't want to drink human blood and partake in the form of cannibalism? Well, we have the right drink for you. Deep red, fruity Sangria is all you need to have a fun time. Sangria seems like a perfect cocktail to have. It is a very good combination of brandy and wine, along with fruits.

**Ingredients:**

- 1 bottle chilled red wine
- 1/2 cup of brandy
- 1 orange
- 1 cup of mixed fruits (strawberries, pineapple, apples, etc.)
- 1 lime
- 1 1/2 tbsp honey
- Ice cubes

**Servings - 6**

**Cooking Time -** 20 minutes

**Instructions:**

Slice the orange into two halves. Squeeze one half into a large bowl or pitcher.

Finely chop the remaining orange and the mixed fruits. Add them to the pitcher.

Pour in the brandy and add the maple syrups. Thrown in the lime slices too.

Pour in the wine and gradually stir the sangria. Add the ice cubes.

To bring out most of the flavors, it is recommended to refrigerate the beverage for 2 hours. But it can be served immediately as well.

## 22. Red Velvet Cupcake for The Vampires

If you love the vampires from this series, then you will definitely love Red Velvet Cupcakes. The beautiful red color reminds you of the vampires' thirst for blood, their fiery personalities, and how deeply they love the ones they consider close. These cupcakes are sweet and delicious. Their recipe is basic and simple. Now you have no excuses not to make them. Read through the instructions and enjoy the batch of cupcakes.

**Ingredients:**

- 1 1/3 cups of cake flour
- 2 tbsp cocoa powder
- 1/2 tsp baking soda
- 1/4 tsp salt
- 1/4 cup of softened butter
- 1 cup of sugar
- 2/3 cup of buttermilk
- 1 egg
- 1/4 cup vegetable
- 1 tbsp red food coloring
- 1 tsp vanilla extract
- 1/2 tsp white vinegar

**Servings Size -** 15

**Cooking Time -** 40 minutes

**Instructions:**

Preheat your oven at 352*F. Grease your muffin or cupcake trays.

Sift the cocoa powder, cake flour, salt, and baking soda in a bowl.

Take out another bowl, pour the buttermilk and add sugar. Whisk it for 5 minutes till the mixture turns creamy.

Add the egg and oil and continue to mix. Pour in the vanilla, vinegar, and red food colorings to the mixture.

Slowly add the dry ingredients, part by part into the wet ingredient bowl. Combine well and make sure no lumps remain.

Pour the batter into your tray to about half the cupcake level. Bake for 15- 20 minutes.

Let them cool down completely before servings. Red velvet cupcakes go well with cream cheese frosting, but you can top it off with any other topping you like.

# 23. Bread and Butter Pudding by Enzo

Now, Enzo may be portrayed as an antagonist but that doesn't mean that he doesn't have his soft times. He could easily turn into one of the characters that make and serve you pudding. Anything is possible if you can imagine it hard enough. Bread and butter pudding is a classic dish from British cuisine. This recipe uses common savory breakfast items to make a sweet dessert pudding. Follow the recipe and enjoy the dish.

**Ingredients:**

- 8 cups of white bread
- 1 cup of raisins
- 3 eggs
- 1 1/2 cups of milk
- 1 cup of thick cream
- 1 tsp of vanilla extract
- 3 tbsp of unsalted butter, melted
- 1/2 cup of white sugar
- 1 tsp of cinnamon powder
- 4 tbsp of extra melted butter to serve

**Serving Size -** 6-8

**Cooking Time -** 35 minutes

**Instructions:**

Preheat your oven at 350*F. Cut the bread into 1-inch square slices.

Whisk the eggs in a large bowl. Pour in the milk and cream and continue to mix.

Add the sugar, cinnamon powder, 3 tablespoons of melted butter, and vanilla. Whisk till all the ingredients are well combined.

Soak the bread pieces along with the raisin in the egg mix for about 3 minutes.

Pour the contents of the bowl into a 2.5-quart baking dish. Pour over 2 tablespoons of melted butter and bake for 30 minutes.

Drizzle the rest of the butter over the pudding. Serve with vanilla ice cream of chocolate sauce.

# 24. Brownies for A Vampire Get-together

Vampires sure do love eating human food though they do not need it to survive. Everyone would probably do the same. Not one would give up a creamy plate of pasta or warm fresh brownies just because they turned into a vampire, right? Speaking of which, brownies are the perfect dessert to make for a large group of people. Ideal for a get-together or parties. The recipe is so easy it will surprise some of you.

**Ingredients:**

- ½ cup of butter
- 1 cup of white sugar
- 2 eggs
- 1 tsp of vanilla extract
- ⅓ cup of unsweetened cocoa powder
- ½ cup of all-purpose flour
- ¼ tsp of salt
- ¼ tsp of baking powder

**Serving Size -** 16

**Cooking Time -** 40 minutes

**Instructions:**

Preheat your oven at 350*F. Spray cooking spray to grease an 8-inch square pan.

Melt the butter and add it to a bowl. Add the sugar and vanilla to it.

Now add the eggs and whisk. Thrown in the dry ingredients, i.e., flour, cocoa powder, baking powder, and salt.

Mix well till all the ingredients combine. Now pour it into a pan. Bake for 25 to 30 minutes.

Allow it to cool a bit once it is ready and serve with whipped cream.

# 25. Stuffed Bell Peppers for Elena's Slumber Party

Elena's parties with her female friends a lot. And surely, she needs to have some tasty dishes in hand. This recipe is perfect for situations like that. Stuffed Bell Peppers is an easy and fun snack. If you are a person who hates bell peppers or capsicum, then this recipe will make you rethink your opinion. The recipe is so simple but the dish tastes amazing. Go ahead and give this dish a shot.

**Ingredients:**

- 4 bell peppers of any color
- 1 lb. ground chicken or beef
- 1 tbsp of chili powder
- 1 tsp of ground cumin
- 1 tsp of garlic powder
- 1 tsp of onion powder
- Salt as per taste
- ¼ tsp of pepper powder
- 10 oz of diced tomatoes
- 4 oz of diced green chiles
- 1 ½ cups of cooked brown rice
- 1 ¼ cup of shredded cheese

**Servings Size -** 4

**Cooking Time -** 30 minutes

**Instructions:**

Fill your instant pot with one to two cups of water. Put the trivet inside the pot.

Wash your bell peppers and slice the top part off. Remove all the seeds and keep only the shell of the bell pepper.

Bring out a bowl and place the ground meat in it. Add the garlic powder, chili powder, salt, onion powder, cumin, and pepper powder. Mix it all together.

Throw in the tomatoes, green chilies, and rice. Continue to mix evenly.

Now mix in 3/4 cup of cheese. Place the bell peppers inside the pot.

Scoop out the filling and fill the bell peppers to the top.

Cover and seal your instant pot. Set on manual mode and cook the peppers for ten minutes on high pressure. Once done, remove the seal to release the pressure.

Sprinkle the rest of the cheese over the peppers, and let it melt in the pot. Serve hot.

# 26. Fake Blood Beetroot Puree

Well, the title explains the recipe perfectly. This is a recipe for making beetroot puree or mash, using beetroot along with potatoes. The deep red color almost resembles blood. But don't worry, this recipe uses no blood of any animal or human. It is an ideal dish to make for a Vampire themed party. The dish is extremely tasty and the recipe is simple and basic. Follow the instructions and you should be good to go.

**Ingredients:**

- 4 lbs. peeled potatoes
- 1 lb. peeled beetroots
- 1/4 cup of butter
- 1 cup of goat cheese
- 1/2 cup of milk
- salt to taste
- pepper to taste

**Servings -** 8

**Cooking Time -** 40 minutes

**Instructions:**

Take out a pot and fill it with water. Boil the potatoes and beetroot till they are soft.

Take them out of the pot and let them cool a bit so that they are easier to work with.

Mash the vegetables using a potato masher or a fork in a bowl. When it is smashed but still a little lumpy, add the butter. Continue mashing.

Pour in the milk to make the mashed potatoes and beetroot smooth.

Crumble the cheese and add it to the bowl. Mix it evenly.

Sprinkle the pepper and salt. Mix well and serve.

# 27. Hot Steak Like Hot Stefan

We have established that Stefan is good-looking. In fact, both the Salvatore Vampire brothers are extremely blessed with looks. Throughout the series, there are a couple of scenes where they show or express that Stefan enjoys cooking. What else could fans ask for? Stefan has it all, a handsome guy who cooks and is a strong vampire. This man definitely deserves a perfect steak on his plate. Follow the recipe and enjoy.

**Ingredients:**

- 2 lbs. ribeye steak
- 1/2 tbsp vegetable oil
- 1 1/2 tsp salt
- 1 tsp pepper powder
- 2 tbsp butter
- 2 cloves of garlic, minced
- 1 rosemary sprig or 1/2 tsp dried rosemary

**Serving Size -** 4

**Cooking Time -** 25 minutes

**Instructions:**

Make sure the steak is clean and dry. Sprinkle salt and pepper to season the steak. Add more seasoning if required.

Place a pan over a medium-high flame, and pour in the oil.

When the oil is heated, place the steak on the pan and sear it on one side for about 3 minutes or till it turns brown in color.

Flip the steak and cook the other side for another four to five minutes.

Sear the other untouched sides for a minute till it browns too.

Bring down the heat and quickly add the butter along with rosemary and garlic.

Tilt and pan and pour the butter over the steak using a spoon. Keep doing it for about a minute or two. Add more butter if needed.

Take the steak off the stove and cut it into strips. Drizzle the butter sauce from the pan over the steak strips and serve.

# 28. Curried Potatoes for Salvatore's Late Dinner

The bond between the Salvatore Brothers is something different. they aren't too close, but neither is their relationship detached. In fact, they share the classic passionate sibling relationship. The one that bonds over home-cooked food at midnight, while just simply talking. Curried Potatoes are made for nights just like these. They are tasty, easy, and healthy to make.

**Ingredients:**

- 1 tbsp oil
- 1 diced onion
- 3 lbs. red potatoes quartered
- 2 tbsp curry paste
- 1 tsp red chile flakes
- 1 tsp garlic salt
- 1 tsp ground black pepper
- 2 cups of vegetable broth
- 2 tbsp cornstarch

**Serving Size -** 6

**Cooking Time -** 30 minutes

**Instructions:**

Heat oil in the instant pot by selecting the sauté option

Stir fry the onions till they are partially cooked for 3 minutes.

Add curry paste, garlic, salt, red chile flakes pepper, broth, and potatoes to the pot. Stir and mix evenly.

Set the Manual mode on an instant pot and cook for 15 minutes. Make sure the pot is covered and sealed. Once done, allow a natural release.

Fill a bowl with hot potatoes. Add cornstarch and mix till it thickens. Serve hot.

# 29. Bloody Wildcat Cooler Mocktail for Vampires

There are a lot of alcoholic drinks and cocktails for vampires in this cookbook. But we must not forget the vampire who simply isn't in the mood for alcohol. There are a lot of deep red mocktails that fit the vampire theme. Wildcat Cooler is one of them. The dark reddish-maroon color is what catches the eye and gives it a bit of a classy look. Try it at home, and see if you like it yourself. Follow the simple instructions carefully and enjoy the beautiful red mocktail.

**Ingredients:**

- 1 cup of fresh blueberries
- 1 cup of water
- 1 cup of sugar
- 1 lemon
- Sparkling water as per requirement
- Ice as per requirement
- Mint leaves to garnish

**Serving Size -** 4

**Cooking Time -** 15 minutes

**Instructions:**

Bring out a saucepan and place it over medium-high flame.

Add the blueberries to the pan along with water and sugar. Allow the water to boil. Meanwhile, squeeze the juice of the lime.

Bring down the heat and let the contents of the pan simmer now.

Allow it to simmer for 10 to 15 minutes. Strain the blueberry jam once it cools down.

Take out your serving glasses and fill them completely with ice. Pour equal amounts of the blueberry jam. Do not stir.

Now pour the lemon juice and then with sparkling water. Give it only one stir if you feel it is needed. Garnish with mint leaves and serve.

# 30. Bloody White Chocolate Bark

How about we move onto something sweet for our favorite vampires. Strawberry White Chocolate bark sounds perfect given the berry fruit barks a bit of a bloody look. These treats are super sweet and tasty. The combinations of strawberries and white chocolate go well together. Try this recipe at home, and I am sure you will crave more.

**Ingredients:**

- 8 oz of white chocolate
- 1/3 cup of frozen dried strawberries

**Serving Size -** 6

**Cooking Time -** 3 hours 15 minutes

**Instructions:**

Place parchment paper on a baking sheet or tray. Chop the dried strawberries finely.

Melt the white chocolate in a bowl over boiling water steam.

Once melted, take it off the heat, and stir well to make sure no chocolate lumps are present.

Add in half the amount of the chopped strawberries. Mix it along with the chocolate.

Pour the melted chocolate smoothly and evenly onto your tray. Sprinkle the remaining strawberries onto the tray.

Refrigerate till it hardens for at least 3 hours. Crack them into pieces to create the bark.

# 31. Puff Pastry for Caroline and Stefan

Now, this may hurt many but Caroline and Stefan were one of the best couples from Vampire Diaries. They are the closest that comes to being ideal, so to say. Puff Pastries are ideal for this couple's romantic date. Actually, it is ideal for any date. They are delicious and surely worth giving a try. Read through this recipe carefully, follow the instructions and enjoy cooling these pastries.

**Ingredients:**

- 8 oz cream cheese
- ¼ cup of powdered sugar
- 1 tsp vanilla extract
- 2 sheets of puff pastry
- Fruits of your choice like strawberries, blueberries, etc.

**Serving Size -** 18

**Cooking time -** 1 hour

**Instructions:**

Preheat the oven to 400*F. Line cookie sheets with parchment paper

Combine the cream cheese, sugar, and vanilla in a bowl until nice and smooth.

Coat your surface with some flour and roll out your pastry sheets

Cut nine squares from each sheet.

Put 2 teaspoons of cream cheese filling in the middle of each square sheet. Place your fruit or berries over the filling.

Place the pastries on the parchment paper and bake them for 20 minutes. The pastries should puff up and turn golden brown.

# 32. Tasty Sandwich for Vampire Elena

Ye, we all know that Elena hated the taste of sandwiches or, well, any human food. It was enough to make her barf up. However, we shouldn't give up that easily. Not when there are so many tasty sandwich recipes out there. This sandwich is made with the sole intent of taste. The recipe is extremely easy to follow. So, go ahead and enjoy making this dish.

**Ingredients:**

- ⅓ cup of julienned or grated carrot
- 1 cup of sliced green cabbage
- 1 spring onion sliced thinly
- ¼ tsp of black pepper powder
- 1 pinch hot chili pepper powder
- ½ tsp of salt
- 2 eggs
- 3 tbsp of butter
- 2 slices of bread
- ½ tsp of sugar
- 2 thin smoked and cooked ham slices
- 1 slice of Cheddar cheese
- 1 tbsp of tomato sauce
- 1 tbsp of mayonnaise

**Serving Size -** 1

**Cooking Time -** 20 minutes

**Instructions:**

Bring out your bowl and add the carrots, cabbage, and green onions.

Season with pepper powder, salt, and hot chili powder. Combine and mix well using your hands.

Crack the eggs into the bowl and whisk them in the bowl along with the vegetables.

Grease the pan with two tablespoons of butter and heat the pan over a medium flame.

Toast the bread slices on the pan till they are crunchy and crisp. Take the slices out and set them aside.

Grease the pan with another tablespoon of butter. Pour in the egg onto the pan. Let it cook for about two minutes.

When it is partially cooked, use a spatula and fold the edges to form a rectangle. Let it cook for some more time, and then cut the omelet into half.

Flip to cook both sides till they are golden brown. Place both the omelet squares onto a bread slice.

Add the smoked ham and cheddar cheese over the hot omelet.

Top it off with some tomato sauce and mayonnaise. Place the other slice over the omelet and serve

# 33. Lime Curd for Lexi

We all need a best friend like Lexi. The friendship she and Stefan had was totally worth cherishing. She even played the role of the wing woman well. A person like her deserves a special treat. Lemon curd is one of the quickest and tastiest recipes you will ever find. It can be used as a dessert all by itself, as well as fillings and toppings for various other desserts. It can be made on the spot anytime, provided you have your ingredients with you. You will surely love this recipe if you are one who goes for zesty flavors.

**Ingredients:**

- 4 large lemons
- 1/2 cup of sugar
- 2 tbsp cornflour
- 1 whole egg
- 3 yolks
- 6 tablespoons butter

**Serving size -** 2

**Cooking Time -** 20 minutes

**Instructions:**

Grate the zest of the lemons, make sure you don't take the white part of it. Now squeeze out the lemon juice and keep it aside.

Whisk the whole egg and the egg yolks together.

In a saucepan, add the lemon juice and zest over low heat. Add the sugar to it

Once it begins to simmer, take out some lemon juice and mix it with cornflour. Add this mixture to the saucepan.

Whisk it slowly. Now add the eggs and the butter to the pan. Stir it slowly till the curd mixture thickens.

Once it thickens, take it off the stove and strain it with a sieve to obtain a smooth curd.

Transfer the curd to your serving bowls or cups and refrigerate them for about 10 minutes before serving.

If you are using the Lemon Curd as a filling, then you can transfer the curd into a piping bag and then refrigerate.

# 34. Skewered Chicken for Salvatore Brothers

As we mentioned before, The Vampire brothers do share their moments. And like most siblings, it is safe to assume they bond over food. Chicken on skewers that are grilled with some tasty, spicy, and sweet sauce sounds perfect, right? This is definitely a recipe one shouldn't miss the opportunity they get to make it. Trust me, it is worth a try.

**Ingredients:**

- 1 1/4 lbs. chicken thigh
- Salt as per taste
- Pepper as per taste
- 1 tbsp oil
- 1 tsp sesame seeds
- 1 tbsp green onion
- 1/4 cup soy sauce
- 1/2 cup of water
- 2 tsp minced garlic
- 2 tsp minced ginger
- 1/4 cup brown sugar
- 1 tbsp honey
- 1 tsp sesame oil
- 1 tbsp rice vinegar
- 1 1/3 tbsp cornstarch

**Serving Size -** 4

**Cooking Time -** 40 minutes

**Instructions:**

Firstly, cut the chicken into small bite-sized pieces. Slice the green onions too.

Place a small saucepan over a medium flame.

Pour the soy sauce, 1/2 cup of water, honey, sesame oil, and rice vinegar into it.

Throw in the brown sugar, ginger, and honey. Bring the liquid to a boil. Turn up the heat if required.

Stir and mix the sauce well.

Mix cornstarch with cold water and add it to the sauce. Keep stirring constantly till the sauce thickens.

Sprinkle salt and pepper over the chicken bits to season them.

Thread them onto a skewer and brush them with oil.

Preheat your grill for about ten to five minutes.

Cook the Yakitori for about 4 minutes per side.

Brush a coat of the sauce over them and grill for another two minutes.

Sprinkle the sesame seed over them and serve.

# 35. Bourbon Mocktail for Damon's Fans

We started this cookbook with a bourbon dish for Damon. Doesn't it seem fitting to end it with a bourbon dish too? Damon is totally handsome and charming, and we need a few bourbon drink recipes up our sleeves if we want his attention. This cocktail recipe comes to our rescue. It is completely easy and we don't have to sweat on the instructions. Just read through the recipe and make it instantly.

**Ingredients:**

- 1/2 tsp of sugar
- 3 dashes Angostura bitters
- 1 tsp of water
- 2 oz of bourbon
- orange peel to garnish

**Serving Size -** 1

**Cooking Time -** 3 minutes.

**Instructions:**

Pour water along with sugar and bitters in a rock glass.

Fill your serving glass with ice. Now stir the contents. Pour in the bourbon and give it another stir.

Serve chilled with a peel of an orange.

# Conclusion

Now, you have a handful of recipes to master. These recipes require only basic ingredients and your regular kitchen utensils and equipment. You can try these recipes anytime, whenever your heart desires to make them. These are a couple of recipes from all around the world, so you can almost consider yourself an expert in those if you could get it right. If you can't turn into a vampire-like Damon, then try making these recipes, and for a moment, pretend you are one. Don't worry, we won't judge.

The plot of the show was great and had terrific seasons. We have grown attached to the characters, and some of us are probably getting nostalgic. Whenever these emotions act up, just come over to the cookbook and cook to our heart's content. Maybe try and experiment, making a few changes to the recipe so that it suits your style. The taste and flavor of most of the dishes are sure to lift and enhance your mood whenever you are feeling low.

# Author's Afterthoughts

Hey there! I'm opening up a direct line of communication with you. I've always been a little shy when it comes to receiving criticisms or general feedback on my work. However, I know that this is a path meant to help my writing journey. I'll absolutely love it if you could take out a few minutes of your time to leave me feedback. I'll like to know what I'm doing right and how I can make my next book better for you. This will mean so much to me.

*Thanks!*

*Lauren P.*

# About the Author

Whatever you think a chef should be, Lauren Perry exceeds your expectations in every way. Based in Atlanta, this culinary professional has always believed that people have different tastes that need to be catered for using creative and organic ingredients. Before diving fully into the catering industry, Lauren worked as a personal chef, where she had the liberty to customize menus based on her experiences and innate skills.

During this time, she mastered the art of creating new recipes and enjoys the freedom to experiment with coming up with something unique. Now a big-time caterer, you can find Lauren at any big or small event that needs a chef with a sound background in catering. Whether it's at weddings, birthdays, or anniversaries, Lauren is always ready with her charming personality and a menu that will tickle the taste buds of all present. However, her first love remains to create new recipes, and she enjoys sharing it with others through her various recipe books.

Made in United States
North Haven, CT
20 November 2021

11332705R00057